Tiny Tinkles Little Musicians Series

BOOK 3

Little Performers SONGS

on 3 Black Keys

Created by **Debra Krol** Pictures by Corinne Orazietti & Melanie Hawkins

This book is dedicated to
all the little people for inspiring me,
and all the BIG people for believing in me.

Copyright © 2022 Tiny Tinkles Publishing Company

All Rights Reserved.

No parts of this publication or the characters in it, may be reproduced or distributed in any form or by any means without written permission from the publisher.

To request permission, or for school visits and book readings,

please visit www.tinytinkles.com

ISBN (Paperback Perfect Bound): 978-1-990563-02-7

First Edition 2022

TIPS TO HELP YOU TEACH USING THIS BOOK

Welcome to the **Tiny Tinkles Little Musicians Series!**

In this 3rd book of the Little Performers collection, your little musician will become more confident in reading music notation. They will be able to easily identify the black key groups, find and play them hands together in many different locations. Your child will also be introduced to single note combinations help to grow more finger strength, dexterity and independence.

NOTE: When playing the patterns and songs in this book, try to keep a steady beat.

When you see
THREEZIE...
pronounced
Three - Zee

PLAY the
THREE
BLACK KEYS

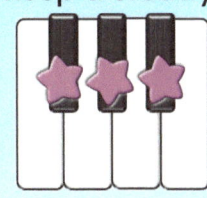

When you see
THESE...
Play THAT
finger

thumb   pointer   middle   ring   pinky

SING while you play the notes! Your little musician will FEEL the beat and rythm of the music.

"PLAY"   "PLAY hold"   "PLAY hold Dot"   "PLAY Great Big Hold"

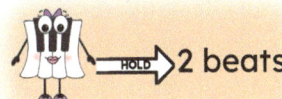 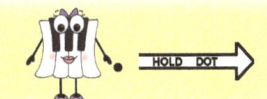 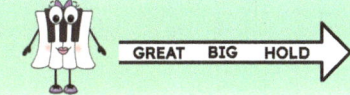

TIPS TO HELP YOU PRACTICE AND LEARN TOGETHER

- Count slowly before you begin.
- Tap the notes and sing LEFT and RIGHT
- Play and sing the WORDS while you play
- Play and sing LEFT / RIGHT while you play
- Play and sing the NUMBERS while you play
- Visit our website if you need help!

For videos, worksheets, teaching tips and more... please visit: **www.tinytinkles.com**

Then, **woosh...**

Threezie jumps playfully through the sky, and plays the pretty notes up **high!**

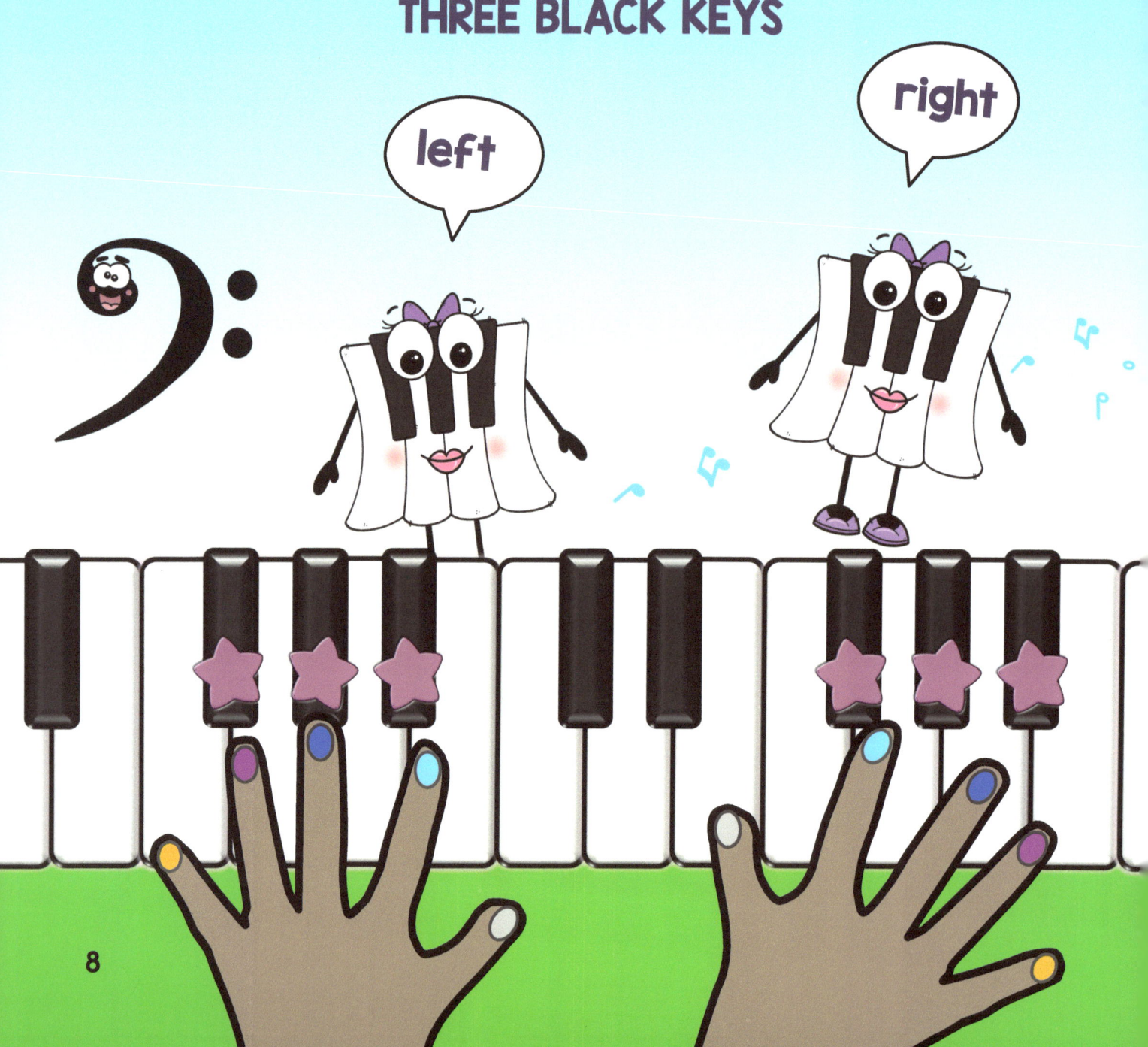

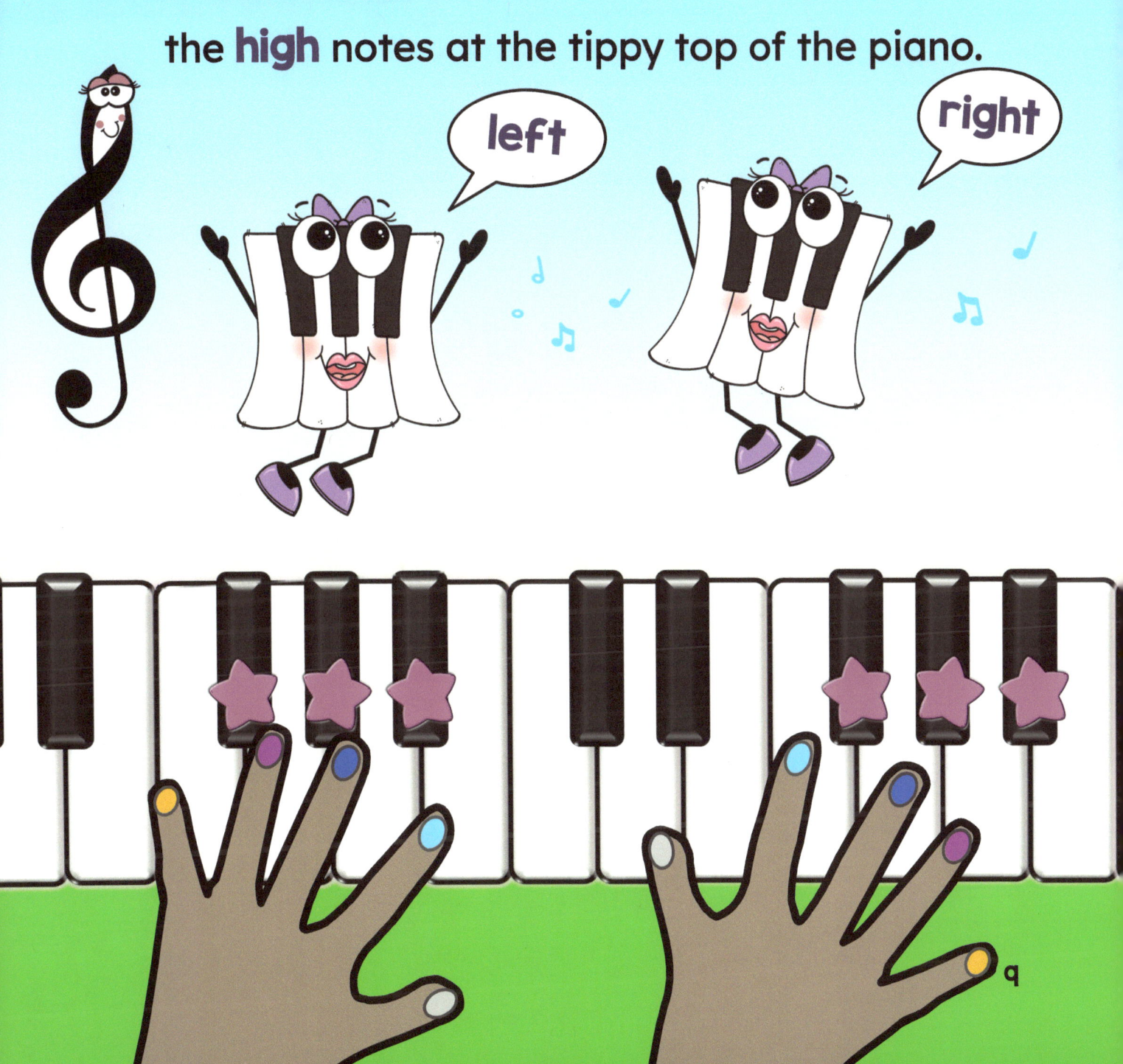

Yipee! A musical adventure on the

THREE BLACK KEYS!

Let's warm up our **Wiggle Friends**.

Wigggle Friend CHEER

Tap tap tap tap tap my LEFT HAND 5 4 3 2 1 hurray!

left

Tap tap tap tap
tap my RIGHT HAND

woosh!

right

Sleepy Puppy
Play **piano soft!** Don't wake up Daisy Dog!

Color a star each time you practice this song.

 Play up **high** on the piano like a lullabye!

Frankie Frog

Frankie loves to hop! Hop with Frankie Frog!

Color a star each time you practice this song.

♪ Play the notes with firm fingertips!

ri bbit Fran ky   Frog.

Rosie Loves to Jump

Can you play **Rosie Rabbit's** notes **staccato** short?

Color a star each time you practice this song.

 Play with a **steady beat**, not too fast.

high high low low

Little Snowman

Imagine a snowball inside your hand! Don't squish it!
Keep your snowball round while you play.

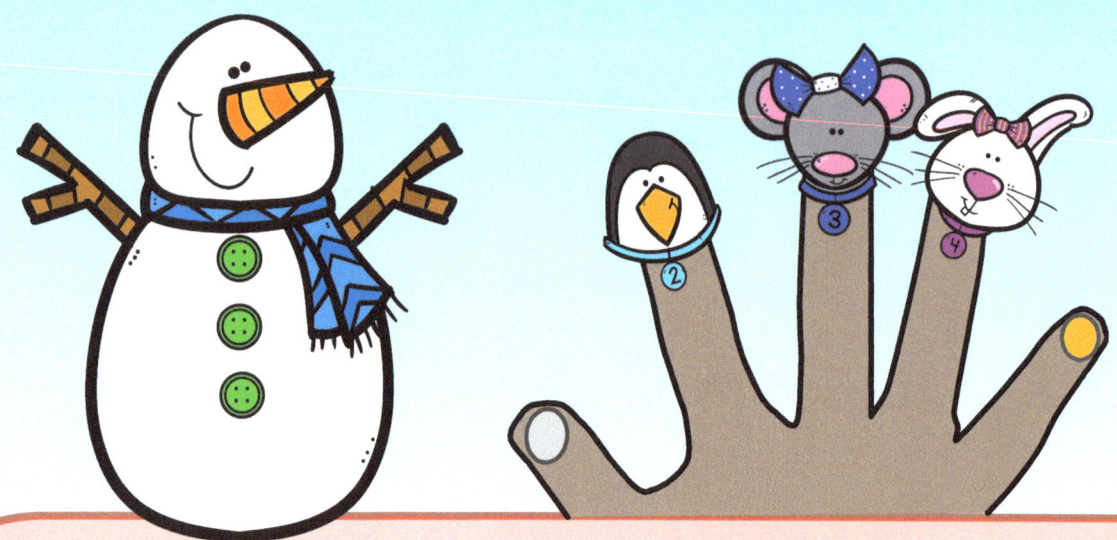

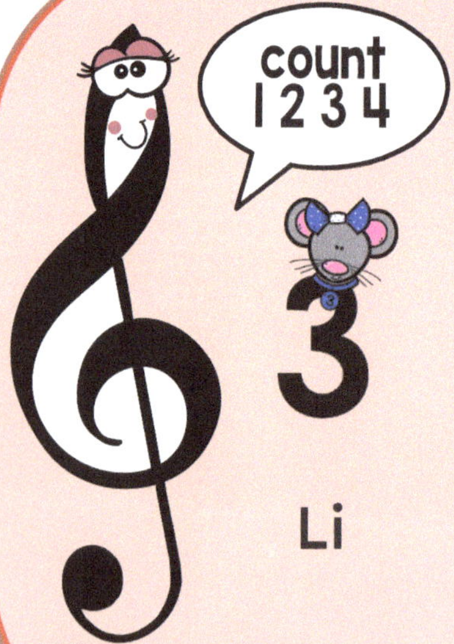

3 3 3 3
Li ttle snow man

2 2 2 2
li ttle snow man

Color a star each time you practice this song.

 Are you playing with firm fingertips?

please   don't   melt.

Color a star each time you practice this song.

☆☆☆☆☆☆☆☆☆☆
☆☆☆☆☆☆☆☆☆☆
☆☆☆☆☆☆☆☆☆☆

 Play the **"BOO!" forte** loud!

Purple Dinosaur

Play the **ROARs forte** loud!

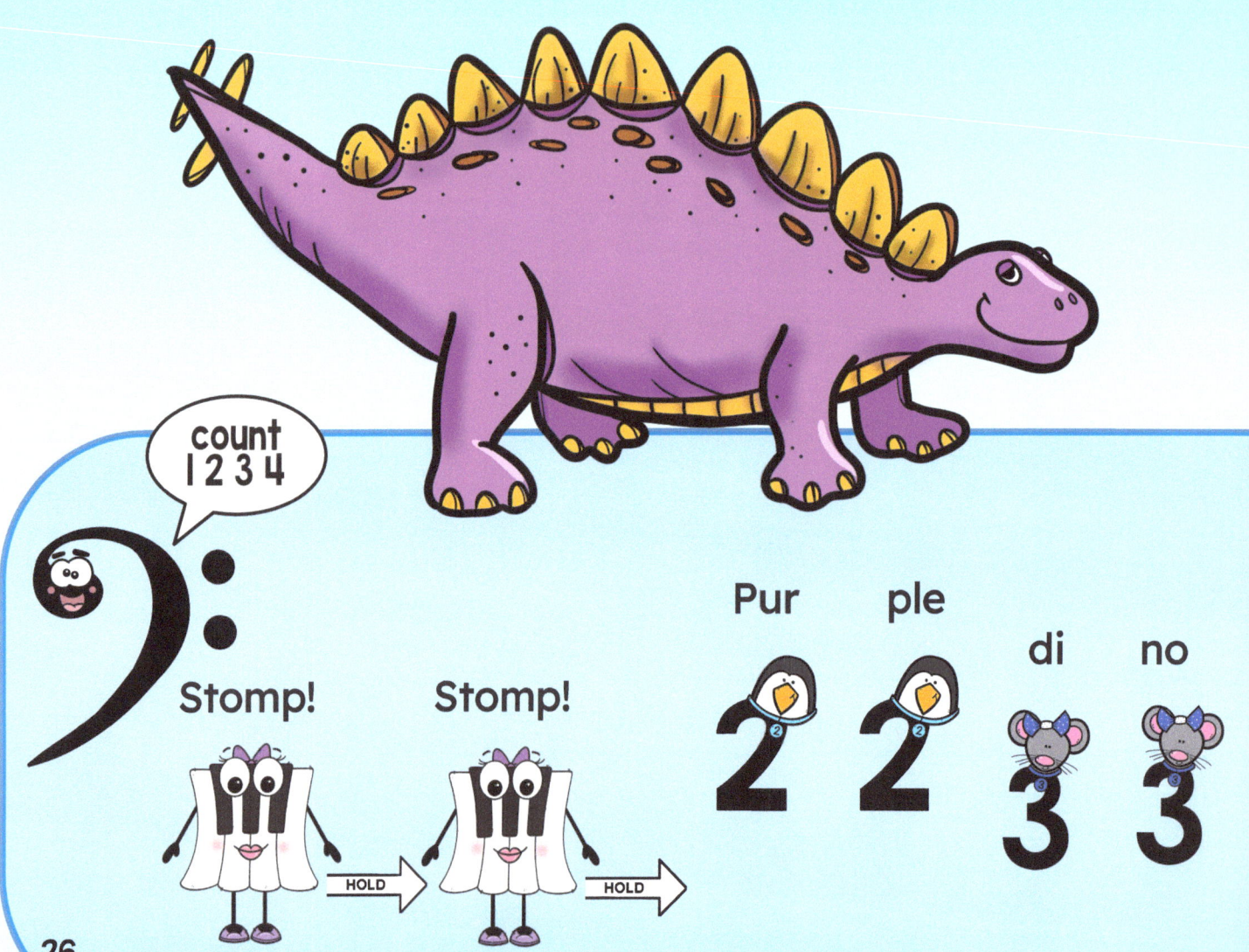

Color a star each time you practice this song.

 Sound like a dino! Play this song **low** on the piano!

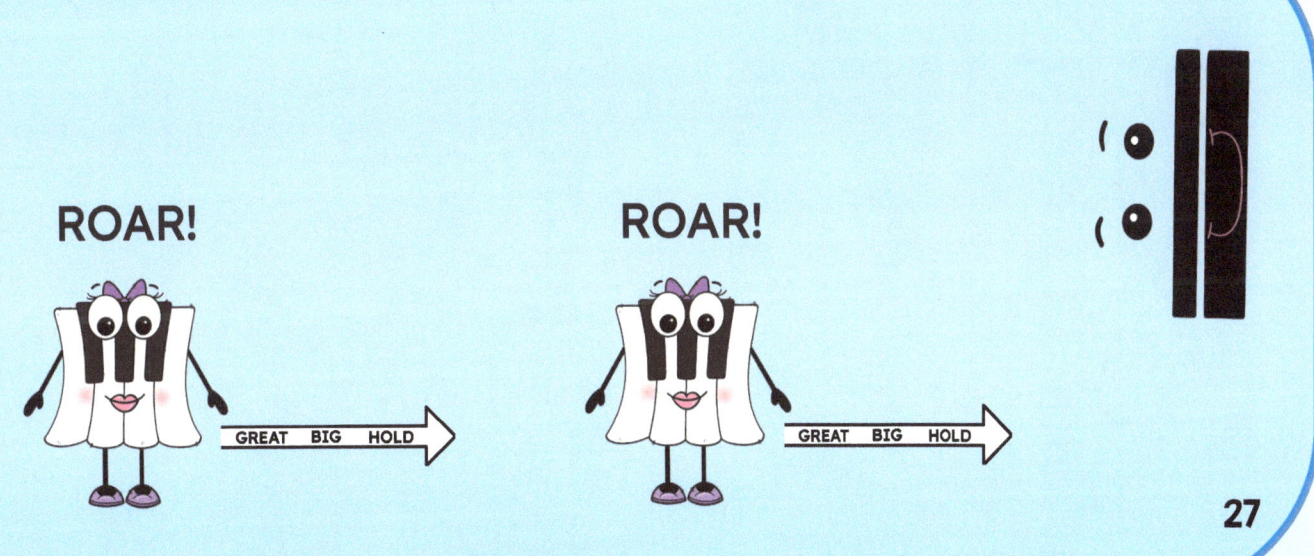

Twirling Around

Pokey Porcupine loves to twirl!

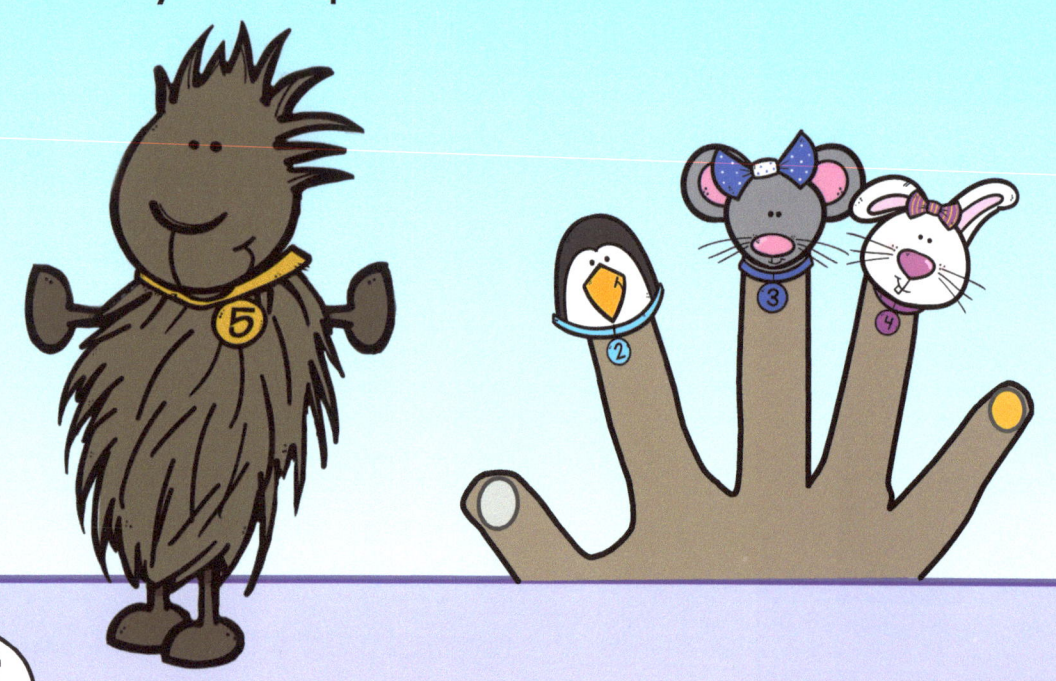

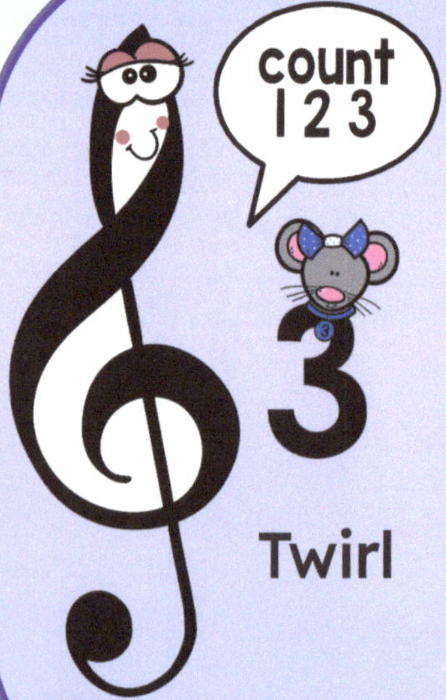

3 3 3 ● HOLD DOT 2 2 2

Twirl ing a round! Twirl ing a

Color a star each time you practice this song.

 Count the holds and dots carefully!

Pony Ride

Hop on, let's go for a ride! Keep it steady.

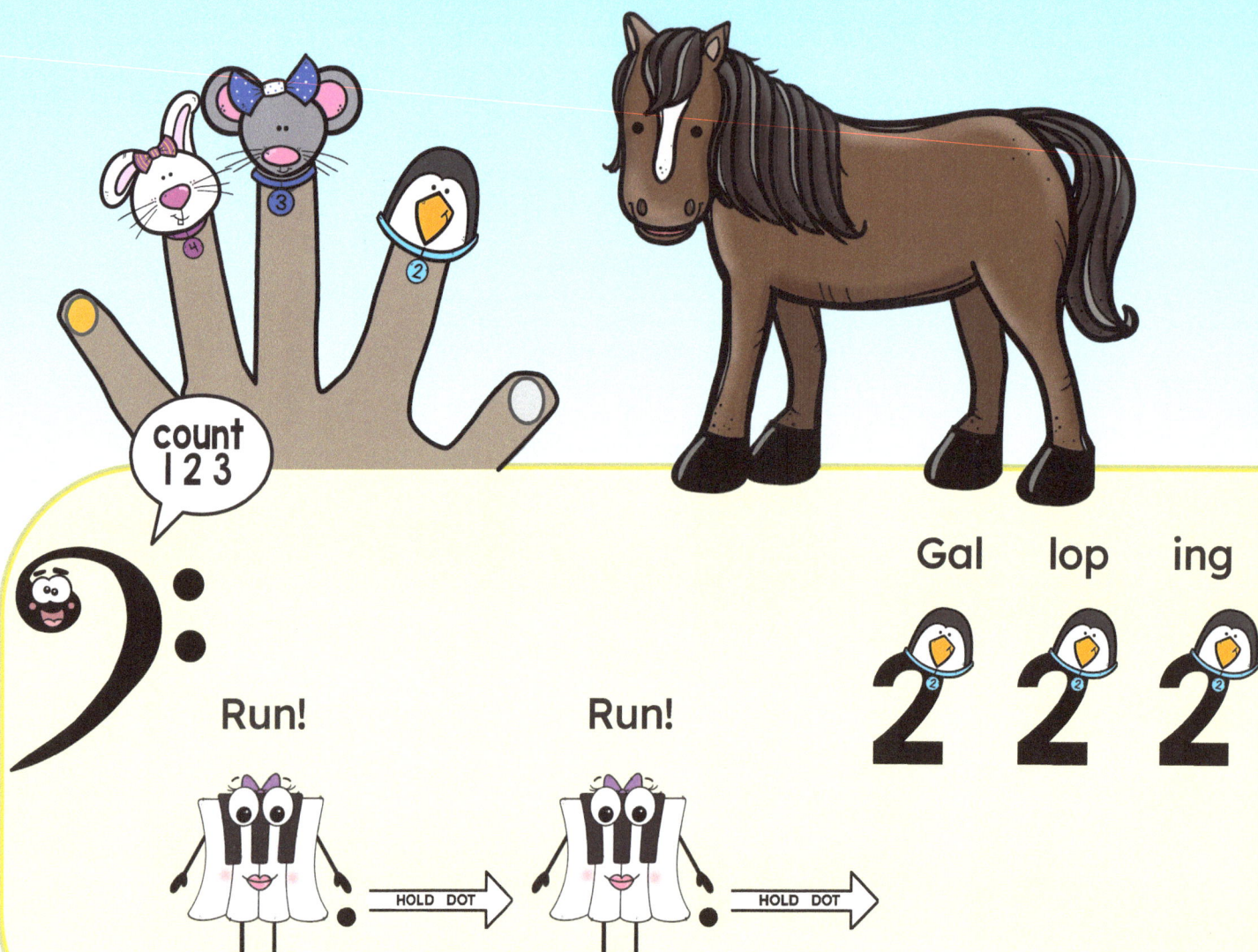

Color a star each time you practice this song.

 Think ahead! The notes are stepping **DOWN.**

The Bumble Bee

Feel the Rhythm! Watch for repeating notes.

Bum   ble   bee

bum   ble   bee

Color a star each time you practice this song.

 Remember to play on your fingertips!

don't   sting   me!

Elly Elephants Song

Wowzers! Watch for repeating notes.

Color a star each time you practice this song.

 Play **forte** loud and **lento** slow.

My Little Ladybug

How many spots can you count on this ladybug?

Color a star each time you practice this song.

 Try this song up **high** and **hands together!**

Pitter Patter

Frogs love water, and they love rain even more!

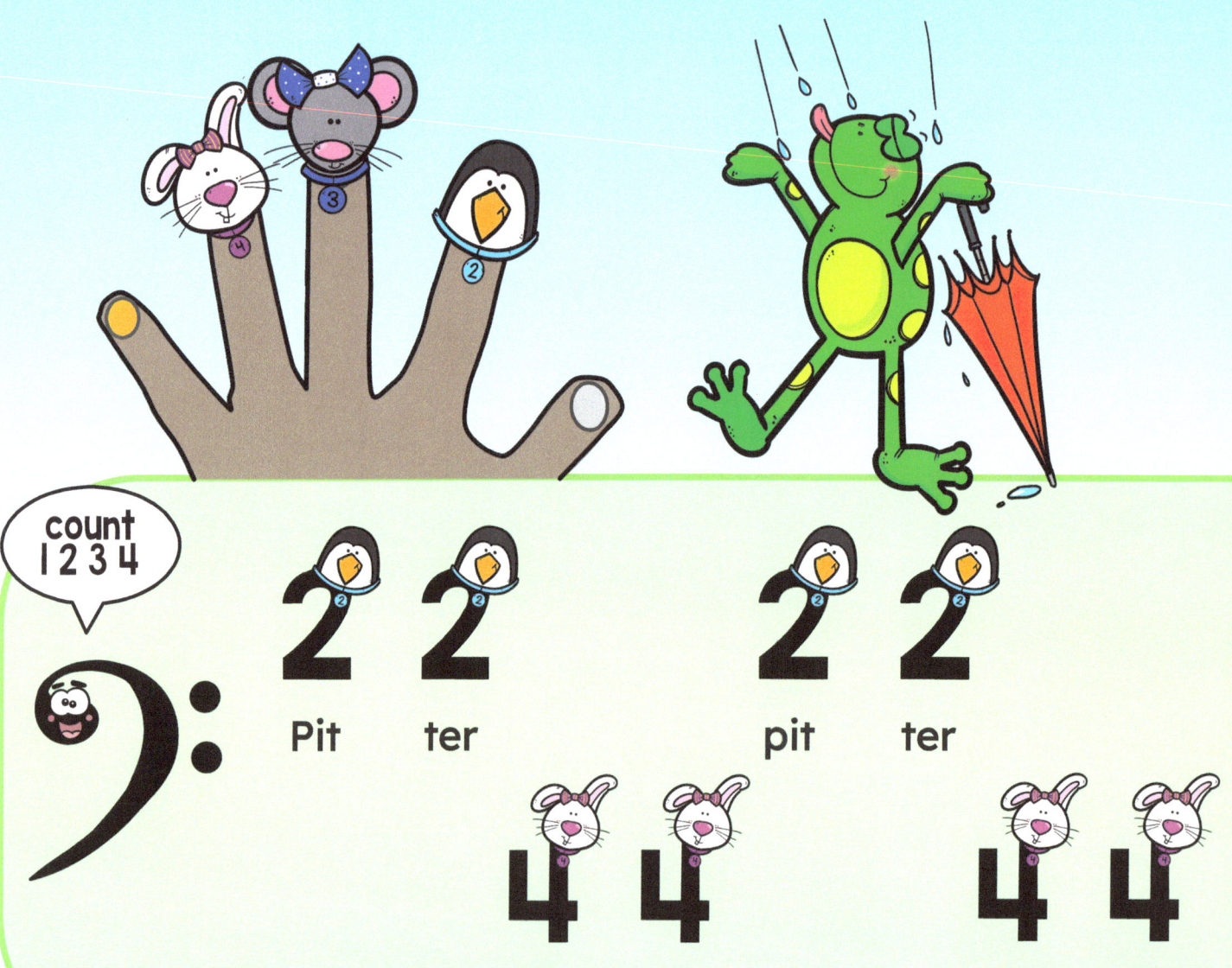

Color a star each time you practice this song.

 Make the pitter patters sound like rain drops by playing them **staccato** short.

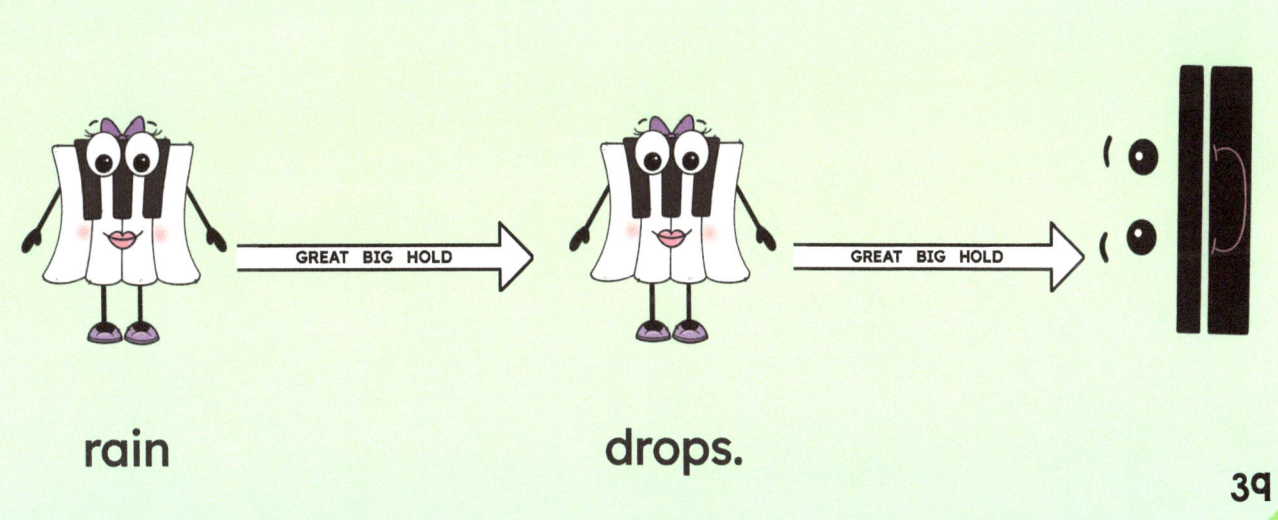

Baby Butterfly

Play this song *piano* soft!

Color a star each time you practice this song.

☆ ☆ ☆ ☆ ☆ ☆ ☆ ☆ ☆ ☆
☆ ☆ ☆ ☆ ☆ ☆ ☆ ☆ ☆ ☆
☆ ☆ ☆ ☆ ☆ ☆ ☆ ☆ ☆ ☆

 Feel the beat, count to 4 before you begin.

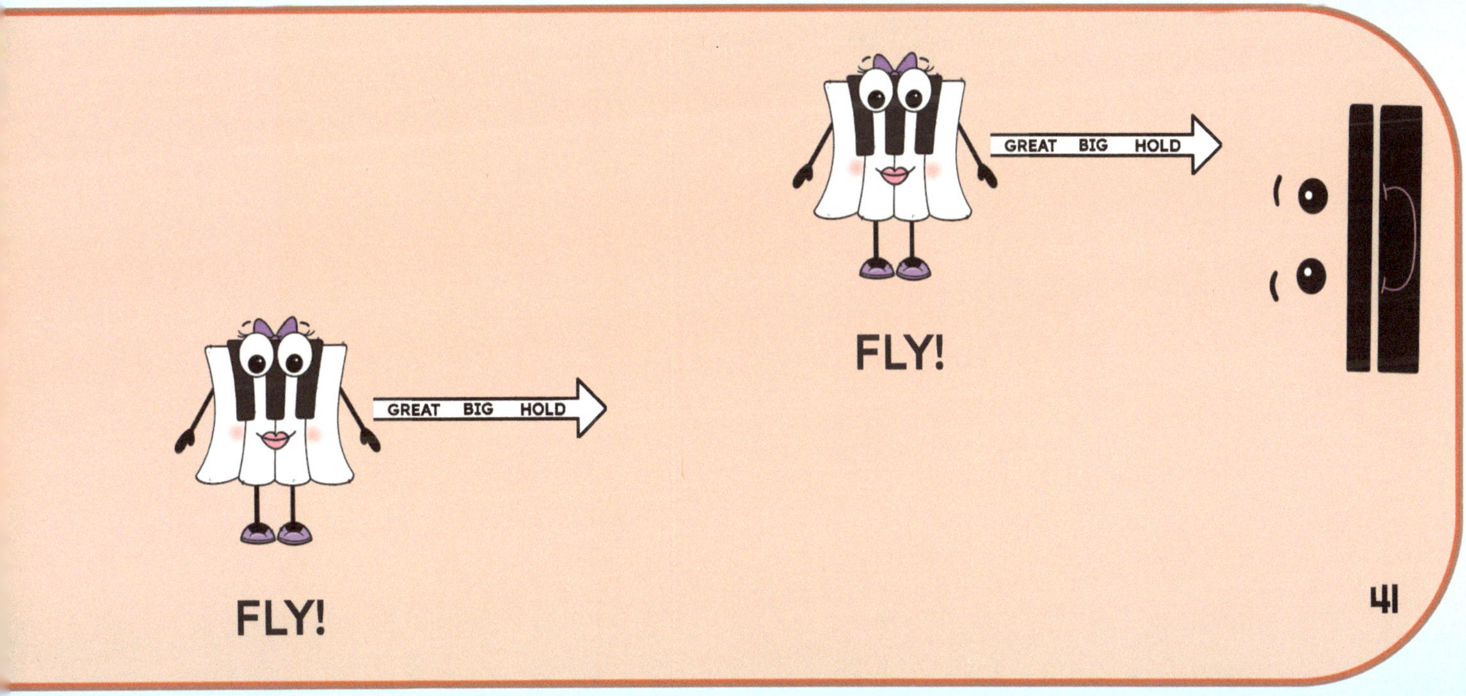

Daddy Butterfly

Don't forget the great big holds!

Color a star each time you practice this song.

 Try flying away on the last **great big hold.**

Dancing Daisy

Daisy Dog Loves to dance!

count 1 2 3 4

3 3 2 2 3 3 2 2
Dan cing Dai sy dan cing Dai sy

4/4

Color a star each time you practice this song.

 Can you make Daisy dance **lento** slow?

Chocolate Ice Cream

What is your favorite flavor?

Color a star each time you practice this song.

 Try playing **hands together!**

The Unicorn Dance

Play this song gracefully! Can you make up a beautiful ending?

Color a star each time you practice this song.

 Try playing **hands together!**

Three Black Keys!
Wow! You've mastered the three black keys! Now try hands together, with the same fingers.

Color a star each time you practice this song.

Can you play this song up **high** and down **low?**

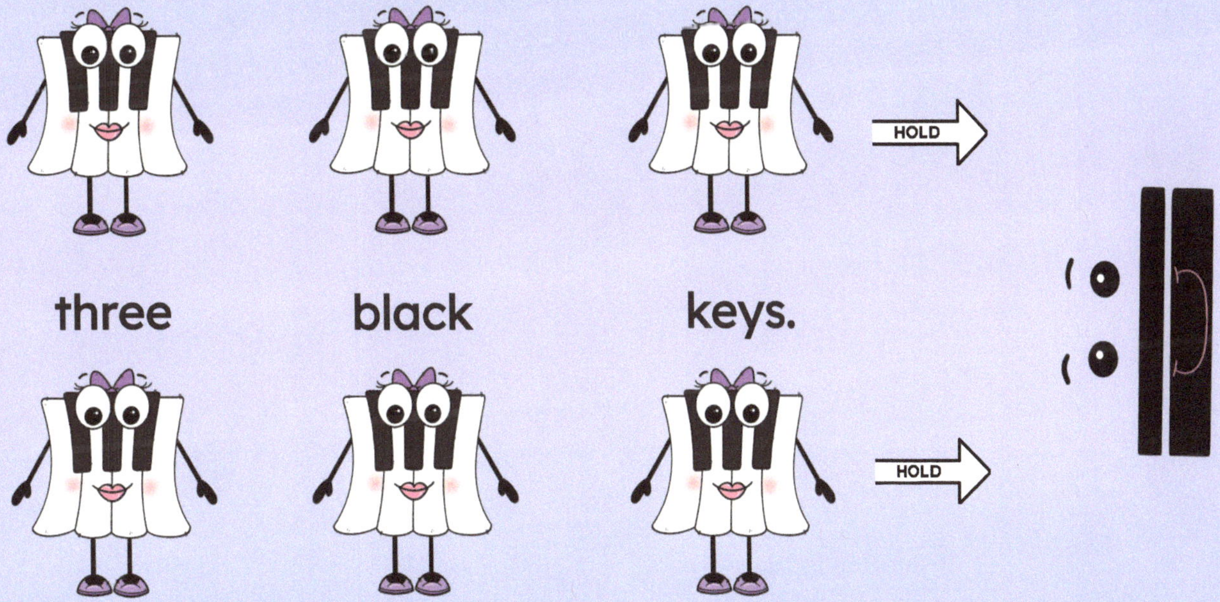
HOLD
three
black
keys.
HOLD

The Rooster

What does a Rooster Say? Sing his song **forte loud!**

Color a star each time you practice this song.

 Can you play this song up **high** and down **low**?

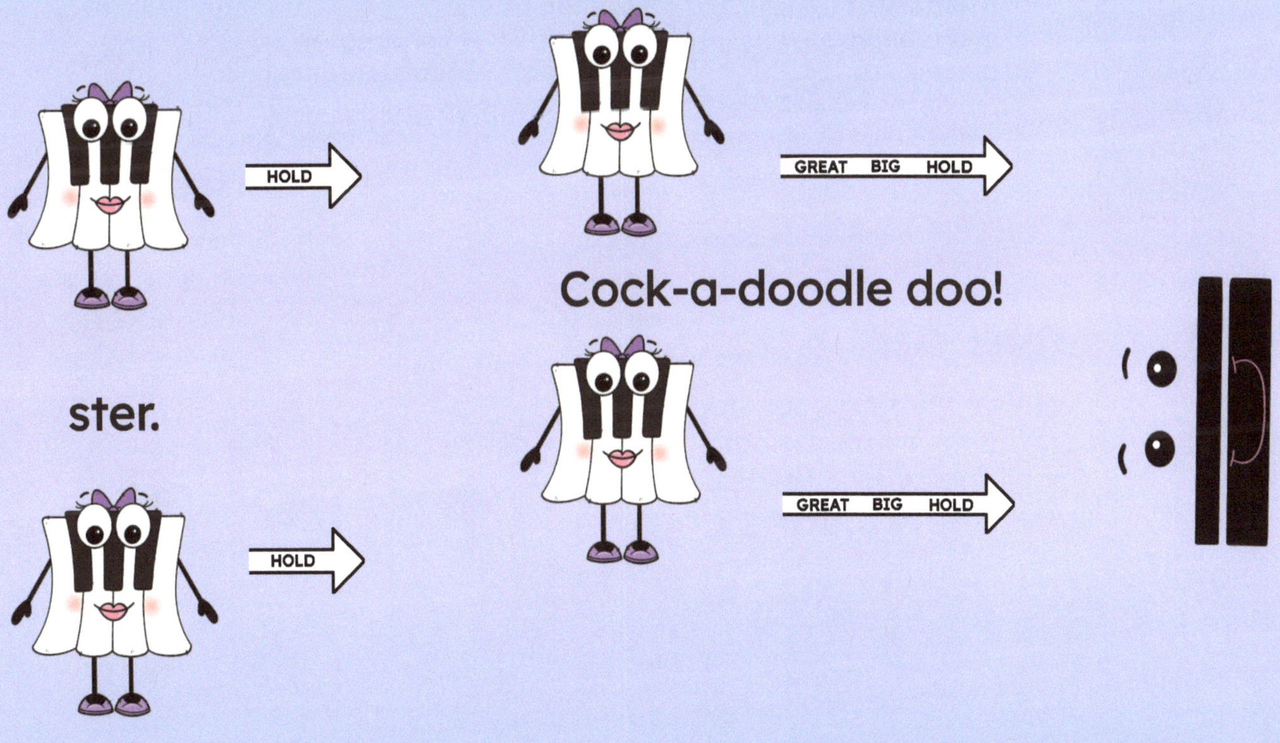

Cock-a-doodle doo!

ster.

ABOUT THE CREATORS

Debra Krol is a BC Registered Music Teacher who specializes in teaching music to babies, toddlers and preschoolers. She is also a children's songwriter and author. Ms. Deb enjoys camping with her hubby, kids, and Daisy Dog, their black and tan coonhound. She loves playing piano, ukulele, guitar and most of all, singing & drawing with all of her little friends!

 Tiny Tinkles Music Studio   tinytinkles

Corinne Orazietti was a preschool and elementary teacher for many years. She saw how her whimsical illustrations added sparkle to her lessons and decided it was time to share her passion for art with others. She now works as a full-time artist at her company, Chirp Graphics, and spends her days drawing cartoon dragons and fairies.

 chirpgraphics   chirpgraphicsclipart

Melanie Hawkins is an author, illustrator, elementary art teacher and mom to seven children! Her family is her greatest source of joy and inspiration. She enjoys camping, swimming, dark chocolate, and movie nights with her family. Melanie is an eternal optimist and wishes that everyone could see the world as she does with all of its beauty, hope and goodness.

 melaniehawkinsauthor.com   inspirejoypublishing

Love our Books?

We love hearing your stories! Please visit our social media pages! For all things Tiny Tinkles, visit
www.tinytinkles.com

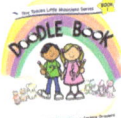  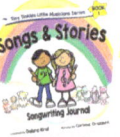 

CONGRATULATIONS!

_____
Student's Name

has completed Little Performers Level 3 in the Tiny Tinkles Little Musician Series.

LEVEL 3

_____
Teacher

_____
Date

www.ingramcontent.com/pod-product-compliance
Lightning Source LLC
Chambersburg PA
CBHW041059070526
44579CB00002B/10